PRAISE FOR *THEN* (

"This compact book is full of insightful wisdom, inspirational experiences, and hard-won humanity delivered by some of the biggest names in American music. Any reader can find something to connect with in this tidy little gem."
—Nickolas Butler, author of *New York Times* bestseller *Shotgun Lovesongs* and *Godspeed*

"Tom Alesia has friends in all the right places. He began chronicling country music during the pivotal point time, when the Garth Brooks camp brought pop-rock marketing sensibilities to Nashville. Tom's conversational style creates a lively thread between then and now with colorful side trips that include Porter Wagoner, John Mellencamp, Doc Watson and a Hank Williams impersonator. *Then Garth Became Elvis* celebrates a meaningful time in American music."
—Dave Hoekstra, Chicago author and documentarian

"Tom Alesia has pieced together a nice narrative of an era in country via the many interviews he's conducted over the years." —Bill Lloyd, **Foster & Lloyd**

"This book is a smart, rapid fire array of quotes, impressions and anecdotes of America's greatest country music stars."
—John Roach, co-screenwriter, Oscar-nominated drama *The Straight Story*

"Tom's glimpses into the lives of these extraordinary artists are fast, fun and compelling. It's a winner!"
—singer/songwriter Becky Hobbs

Then Garth Became Elvis

★ ★ ★

A Country Music Writer's Journey with the Stars, 1985–2010

TOM ALESIA

GRISSOM PRESS
Chicago, Illinois

GRISSOM PRESS
Chicago, Illinois

Printed in the United States of America
Cover design by Sara DeHaan

ISBN 978-1-0879-8929-7

CONTENTS

Chapter 3: Garth, Elvis and Other Icons

Chapter 4: Songwriting and Albums

Chapter 5: Defining Country

Chapter 6: Names and Looks

Chapter 7: Humble and Kind

Chapter 8: Big, Big Hits

Chapter 9: Connecting

Chapter 10: Hardships and Tragedies

Chapter 11: In Concert

Sarah Buxton (2007)   118
Alan Jackson (1998)   118
Doc Watson (2003)   119
George Strait (2001)   119
Dixie Chicks (2000)   120
Aaron Tippin (2001)   121
Hank Williams Jr. (1991)   122
Shania Twain (1998)   123
Kitty Wells (1994)   124
Johnny Cash (1986)   125
Merle Haggard (1993)   126
Ralph Stanley (2001)   127

ABOUT THE AUTHOR

Tom Alesia won the national Music Journalism Award for two feature articles about the Fendermen, a one-hit wonder with their 1960 rockabilly cover of country legend Jimmie Rodgers' "Mule Skinner Blues." He also was a finalist for the award and earned four first-place honors, including two for arts criticism, from the American Association of Feature Editors. His writing has appeared in newspapers nationwide, *TV Guide Magazine* and the book *Tasty Morsels*, a short fiction anthology. Find his work at TomWriteTurns.com. A 35-time marathon finisher and a cancer survivor since 1998, he lives in Madison, Wisconsin, with his wife, Susan. They have a son, Mark.

PREFACE

Each interview was done by me between 1985 and 2010. It captures many country stars during their heyday as well as critical favorites, several legends and industry notables. I attended all of the concerts described without attribution in Chapter 11.

INTRODUCTION

I grew up in a large, concrete Chicago suburb in the shadow of the city's O'Hare Airport. I didn't fish, hunt or drive a pick-up truck...I don't remember *seeing* a pick-up truck. Vacation drives put my family in small towns, where we snickered at the slow life. I stepped on my first working farm at age 22.

In other words, when I left for college at Indiana University in fall 1984, country music and many of its subjects seemed as close to me as the moon. Aside from a few country crossovers to pop music—middling tunes by Kenny Rogers or Eddie Rabbitt—my exposure was shamefully limited.

That changed quickly when I stumbled on an artist-friendly country radio station in Bloomington, Indiana. The airwaves' floodgates opened to Rosanne Cash, Dwight Yoakam, Kathy Mattea, Randy Travis (oh, that baritone), Sweethearts of the Rodeo, K.T. Oslin, Foster & Lloyd, Rodney Crowell, Patty Loveless, The O'Kanes, k.d. lang, Steve Earle, Lyle Lovett and more. Most of them were singer-songwriters with talent to burn.

And then I dug deeper, attending a 1986 Johnny Cash show at the quaint Little Nashville Opry in Nashville, Indiana. Not long before that was my first Marty Stuart concert in the same theater. And hearing Vern Gosdin's 1988 hit, "Set 'Em Up Joe," led me to his past treasures and other stellar veterans.

Even rock added some twang. Lone Justice, with vocalist Maria McKee as alt-country's first queen, sent critics into a tizzy. Milwaukee's BoDeans provided delicious rootsy rock; and Bloomington resident John Mellencamp, whose woodsy mansion sat a few miles from campus, gained remarkable fame. (It was Mellencamp who made a surprise encore appearance at Lone Justice's local club gig to send an already phenomenal show into euphoria.)

By 1989, Clint Black and Garth Brooks appeared with cowboy hats firmly in place and ready to steer the country genre with many of the aforementioned acts along for the ride.

Yes, the year 1985 was a good time to start writing about country music for the school paper. I reviewed these acts and, better still, I interviewed many of them for newspapers and magazines.

This book concentrates on country music's renaissance and revival and its heroes and hardships: 1985 to 2010. That's when every living icon seemed to keep touring: Jones, Willie, Merle, Cash, Kitty Wells, Ray Price, Ralph Stanley, Patsy Montana, Earl Scruggs and Doc Watson. And yes, at the same, Shania Twain sent country music into another universe; her energy in concert alone could levitate a tour bus. Later, Miranda Lambert broke through. So did Sugarland. Eric Church, too.

And they talked, telling me fascinating stories and offering insight. I cherish these interviews, and I appreciate the artists, the famous to the infamous and the fringe acts to the devoted impersonators.

My journalism career wound through South Bend, Indiana; Wausau, Wisconsin; Milwaukee; and Springfield, Illinois, where I talked to central Illinois native Alison Krauss, just age 19, about her first Grammy nomination. She proceeded to win 27 times.

I've stayed the longest in Madison, Wisconsin, where my palate extended to bluegrass and folk. But each place that I've lived enjoyed enthusiastic country audiences, which crossed over to folk and pop. For this book, I included Don McLean talking about "American Pie"; Peter Yarrow of Peter, Paul and

Mary displaying activism at its most ardent level; and Arlo Guthrie speaking directly about the 1960s.

There's even hair-metal singer Sebastian Bach of Skid Row, raving about how much he enjoyed hearing Carrie Underwood cover the Skid Row hit "I Remember You" on a 2007 concert tour.

I was inspired by unfiltered openness during lengthy interviews with Wynonna, K.T. Oslin, Randy Travis, Steve Earle, Doc Watson and Joe Diffie. The Oak Ridge Boys' William Lee Golden allowed me to shift from music questions to discuss his nearly 21-inch-long beard. Alison Krauss gave me five interviews during one frantic decade.

Country acts always courted radio and would appear at small clubs, county fairs and even bowling alleys. Darryl Worley stood in a club's kitchen, moments before going onstage, to discuss his hugely popular single that dominated country radio in 2003.

Spurred by the desire to add a token to country music's rich tradition, I collected copies of nearly 1,000 stories that I wrote. I chiseled at the articles, seeking the best stories, quotes, observations and humor. What follows are the icons and the wanna-bes, the sudden superstars and the critics' favorites. Each of them unguarded and honest, just like the best country tunes.

Enjoy.

Tom Alesia
October 2021

CHAPTER 1

Sudden Fame
or Slow Rise

Wynonna

— 2004 —

"I was 18 years old and supporting 50 workers with my career. That's not normal. I never met my father. I did not know who he was until I was 30, and he died before I knew his name. There's a lot of pain and loneliness about being famous and young and in a hotel room by yourself.

"Let me make this clear: I'm not saying I wouldn't do it over again. I just would have done it differently. I would have taken better care of myself. I tried to take care of others. Ask any mother who has children how tired she is at the end of the day because she's taking care of everyone else."

Tim McGraw

In 1993, McGraw was another young "hat act" country singer with video-ready good looks and expectations of stardom. Then his debut album tanked. Big time.

"I was close to getting dropped. Someone at the record company stood up for me and asked that I be able to cut another record."

The next record, "Not a Moment Too Soon," sold more than 6 million copies.

"I really thought I missed the big wave of country. And I knew there was nothing else I could do for a living."

Mary Chapin Carpenter

—— 1998 ——

A fledgling country singer on a nationally televised awards show in 1990, Carpenter performed a witty tune that she wrote about the genre's many hopefuls called "Opening Act." The song described the overwhelming struggle to become part of country music's hierarchy, which isn't known for its sense of humor.

"Just before I went on stage, Ricky Van Shelton's manager, who knew what I was going to do, said, 'That was a nice career you had going, Carpenter.' I thought the audience would trash it or they'd shake their heads thinking, 'I don't get it.'"

Instead, they gave her a standing ovation.

"I was totally unprepared," she said.

Her record company, however, sensed a way to get her on country radio overnight by having her record the song.

She declined. "The song only worked in a certain context."

Then, on her own terms a year later, country radio embraced Carpenter's music, and she enjoyed a string of hits, including "Down at the Twist and Shout," "I Feel Lucky" and "Passionate Kisses."

K.T. Oslin

—— 1990 ——

Oslin returned to Nashville in the mid-1980s singing her own material at showcases and using her extensive background as a New York theater actress and vocalist.

"I have been trained for performing. I'm not out of the chute saying, 'Golly, I'm only used to singing for my family.' I'm a specialist."

RCA Records executive Joe Galante signed Oslin and then warned her: "This will either work big or not at all."

Within three years, Oslin won three Grammy Awards and sold more than a million copies each of her two albums — an unprecedented accomplishment for a country music newcomer in her late 40s.

Bryan White

A boyishly handsome singer, White soared to fame as quickly as fireworks launching. While signing autographs after a show in Florida, White, then 22, was approached by a young woman wearing a wedding dress.

"She was 17 or 18 and showed up with her parents. She hands me a Bible, and the Bible has my name and her name written on it. She says, 'Will you marry me?' I said, 'Are you crazy?'

"I was shocked by it. I took a picture with her and looked at her parents. I said, 'Are you guys kidding? Surely, this is a joke. I don't even know her.'" He paused. They were serious, he thinks—and White was spooked by the incident.

"I said (quickly) to them, 'Thanks for coming, goodbye.'"

Neal McCoy

He kicked around Nashville and his native Texas for 14 years before he notched a hit single. At 38, he enjoyed a hot streak that began in 1994. But what was he doing at age 21?

"Gosh, I was selling ladies shoes. I had just gotten out of junior college. I just moved to Longview, Texas, and I was working in a mall selling shoes."

He added with a laugh: "I'd rather have been a star at the time."

Tanya Tucker

Reflecting on her teen stardom in the early 1970s, she was ambivalent.

"I went to a lot of places," she said, "but I didn't see much."

Kix Brooks, Brooks & Dunn

—— 1994 and 2003 ——

"It's beyond our wildest dreams. We've worked so hard every day keeping up with this thing, too. In two years, we've gone from having our band and crew and equipment on one bus to traveling with three full buses and five full semis.

"If this happened to me in my 20s, I hate to think how I'd be behavin' now. I have a real appreciation for what a long shot this is."

"Our success seemed very unreal at the start. It still does. I can remember our management sitting down with us after our third hit ('Neon Moon') and putting together a three-year plan. We're like, 'What? Three years? What are you talking about? How about next week?' We still kind of think that way."

Sugarland

Eating humble pie on their way up:

> Side stage lineup, Taste of Madison (Wisconsin)
> Pie eating contest, 1 p.m.
> Sugarland, 2 p.m.

Randy Travis

In 1985, he cooked catfish, washed dishes and sang tender ballads at one of the Music City's numerous restaurant/clubs. A year later, the soft-spoken singer's debut release, "Storms of Life," a country-roots album, was on its way to selling two million copies.

Travis' second album, "Always & Forever," topped its predecessor's sales figures and spawned the classic "Forever and Ever, Amen."

"It seems amazing that it happened so quickly. It seems like no time ago that we started working the road. Now, we have 50 people working for us. That's hard for me to imagine. That's incredible."

CHAPTER 2

Honors and Perspective

Don Reid, Statler Brothers

The squeaky-clean Statler Brothers' first hit single, a country-pop tune "Flowers on the Wall," toppled several heavyweight nominees to win 1965's Grammy award for best contemporary performance by a group . . . a rock 'n' roll category.

They beat the Beatles ("Help!").

They beat the Supremes ("Stop! In the Name of Love").

And they beat "Wooly Bully" and "Mrs. Brown, You've Got a Lovely Daughter."

Yes, the homey Statler Brothers topped the Fab Four—in their prime—for a rock award.

"We were shocked," said Reid, who was 18. "We were brand new on the scene and didn't think we had a chance."

During that same 1965 Grammy ceremony, Reid felt overconfident about "Flowers on the Wall" propelling them to win another category: best new country and western group.

"When you're green, you're expecting everything, so the success of `Flowers on the Wall' wasn't a surprise. You're young and stupid, and you think this could happen to anybody."

Miranda Lambert

Lambert's debut album, "Kerosene," took more than a year to sell one million copies despite enthusiastic live support. Its follow up, "Crazy Ex-Girlfriend," followed a similar slow but steady path.

Her biggest career boost, she said, occurred when "Crazy Ex-Girlfriend" won the Academy of Country Music's award for best album.

She was 24 and spoke while she sat on then-boyfriend Blake Shelton's tour bus.

"I was totally shocked. Very, very surprised. It's changed the way I perceive myself and the way people perceive me. I think it helped me get a Top 10 single. It made me not need to prove myself anymore. The industry gets me and likes my music."

Since then, she's won 27 more ACM awards.

15

Patsy Montana

—— 1989 ——

Tiny and spry Montana, in full cowgirl performance attire, scanned a traveling country music museum exhibit, a portion of which was dedicated to her career.

A 25-year veteran of Chicago's "WLS Barn Dance" radio show, Montana became the first female country singer to sell more than one million records, thanks largely to her hit, "I Wanna Be a Cowboy's Sweetheart," in 1936.

Montana, 75, reacted humbly when she spotted her white "Barn Dance" cowboy boots.

"I hope," she said with a grin, "that they still don't have manure on 'em."

John Hiatt

He is 0-for-9 at the Grammys.

"Isn't that wild? I quit going. Guy Clark and I talked about it. I said, 'I hate going out there and losing.' He said, 'I'm the same damn way. I don't go.' I said, 'OK, I'm not going.'"

(Postscript: Guy Clark won his first and only Grammy in 2013 after being nominated 12 times. Hiatt remains winless.)

Greg Brown,
singer/songwriter

—— 1996 ——

"In America, there's this feeling that everything has to be getting bigger and bigger—more, more, more. That's not my outlook on my life and my career. I've developed a nice audience around the country that I enjoy playing for. It's not huge, but the music I like, acoustic music and blues, shines well in a small club or theater."

Vince Gill

Gill has won more than a few dozen awards, including many Grammys and piles of country industry honors. All that hardware could cover a rec room's walls.

"It's pretty neat," Gill said.

Wait, Vince, you mean all the awards are in one room?

"No, no," he said with a laugh. "They're spaced out here and there. A couple of them are in the closet. I tease people that I use them for hood ornaments. I feel pretty blessed by it all."

Les Paul, guitarist

—— 2004 ——

Paul won a Grammy Award with Chet Atkins for best country instrumental performance in 1977 from co-presenter Dolly Parton.

"When Chet called me, he said he would play the violin and sing and I would play banjo and the harmonica. The first night in Nashville when we recorded, we both thought it sounded awful.

"I said, 'Why don't we do what we're known for? You play your guitar and I'll play mine.' That worked."

CHAPTER 3

Garth, Elvis and Other Icons

Garth Brooks

—— 1990 ——

On April 7, 1990 at Farm Aid IV in Indianapolis, I wanted to interview one of the many little-known acts on the lengthy bill. Anyone, really. Backstage, I spotted a husky, small-town Oklahoma singer standing alone, his chest still heaving after playing two songs in the sold-out Hoosier Dome.

We shook hands.

He said the gig was, by far, the biggest one he had ever done. He usually played county fairs and clubs. Marveling at the event's enormity, he rattled off names of the lineup's country and rock superstars.

"I'll be down-to-earth honest with you, pardner," Garth Brooks continued. "I'm just damn flattered to be here."

Somewhere between that point and now, Brooks became the second bestselling artist in history.

Becky Hobbs

—— 2021 ——

One week after Garth's 1990 Farm Aid appearance, he co-headlined two shows in one night with Hobbs at a remote central Illinois theater called Nashville North. Hobbs, a relentless touring act who never gained full traction on the country radio charts, clearly remembered that gig.

"I was struck by his vibe; he was humble and respectful. I didn't know he would become the superstar that he is—probably because I had learned enough about the music business to know how unpredictable it was. I knew Garth could write songs, choose great songs and be a great entertainer. But he had not gone 'full Garth' yet."

Garth also opened for Hobbs on Sept. 5, 1986, when Brooks was a popular local act in Stillwater, Oklahoma, after he failed to generate any interest during his first move to Nashville. The show was at a rowdy club called Binks in Stillwater. Hobbs changed for the show in the women's washroom because there was no backstage.

"And I put on my show boots in the kitchen; there was more room."

Garth Brooks

In summer 1990, Brooks performed as the substitute opening act at the Illinois State Fair for headliner K.T. Oslin. It rained all day, causing officials to close the muddy horse racing track between the stage and the permanent seats. Instead of the usual standing-room crowd in front of the stage, about 2,000 people sat in a dumpy grandstand suited for seven times that number.

"You guys seem 800 yards away," Garth said.

Upset with the distance between the fans and the stage, he took a cordless mike, stepped into the ankle deep mud and stomped across the slop to perform several songs.

The crowd went bonkers.

Garth Brooks

—— 1992 ——

After a press conference, Brooks met contest winners from a St. Louis radio station. Their reaction startled Brooks. One teenager wept after she received a hug from Brooks, and another trembling fan offered him an affectionate poem. Adult fans climbed platforms and scrambled feverishly to grab Brooks posters.

Then a young man addressed Brooks.

"You're about the closest thing to a hero I've ever had; you and my Dad," the man said. "I don't have anything to give you that you can hold in your hand. But I have something to give you that's heartfelt and that's my loyalty."

Brooks shook hands with the man and said gently, "I hope you never know the real me."

"I don't think I redefined country music. It's thanks to the people at Billboard who began to compile its album charts by computer instead of asking store owners what is selling. Country is finally getting some respect."

Kathy Mattea

"Garth used to sing demos for my husband [songwriter Jon Vezner] and he said: 'He's a hyper guy. I don't know if I can focus with him or not,'" Mattea said laughing.

"Garth was a young, struggling performer who always came around the studio—then he turned into this 'Elvis.' It was an absolutely amazing thing to watch."

Clint Black

Garth Brooks and Black released their debut albums on the same week in 1989. Black rose to prominence quickly, and Brooks slowly climbed the country hierarchy in his first 18 months as a major label artist before reaching star status.

"Back when I first came out, there was stuff I read from Garth's interviews that there was a rivalry between us. I tried to stay away from that, but it seemed to stick with us. To see us together now, you'd never sense any rivalry. All we do is enjoy each other."

Bill Malone, historian

—— 1997 ——

As a young concertgoer, Malone was infuriated at a mid-1950s show when performer Hank Snow cut short his set because the bill also featured a young, rising star. Malone told the story with a laugh because the rising star was Elvis Presley.

Still, "I was an old-time country music fan even then. I thought Elvis was going to destroy it."

Jimmie Dale Gilmore

—— 1994 ——

At age 10, Gilmore saw a double bill of Johnny Cash and Elvis Presley in Lubbock, Texas, in October 1955.

"It was probably one of the turning points of my life. Elvis was a madman on stage, but I was equally impressed with both of them. That was the night I decided I was going to be a musician."

Billy Walker

—— 1997 ——

In 1954, Walker co-headlined a show with Slim Whitman in Memphis when a newcomer opened for them.

"The promoter asked if it was okay if he put this kid on before us. We said fine, and I watched him from the side of the stage and, man, he really knocked the crowd out."

The "kid" was Elvis Presley.

Walker, nicknamed The Tall Texan, later paid Elvis $150 to perform as part of the Billy Walker Show for one week on the road in January 1955. Elvis performed a mix of country, gospel and R&B.

"I remember thinking, 'He's really different, and he's got something.' But he got that shake in his leg from being nervous on stage."

★ ★ ★

Willie Nelson was new to Nashville and lived with Walker in 1960.

"I knew him from Texas so when he came to Nashville I asked him where he was living. He said, 'Out in the old Buick.' I said, 'Get your gear and come to the house.' He stayed for three months, and he wrote 'Funny How Time Slips Away' for me."

Nelson also often reminded Walker about the day job that Walker helped him get: selling encyclopedias.

"We always joke about that."

Willie Nelson

— 1992 —

At a Branson theater in 1992, Nelson spent most of his spring and summer performing for the tourist hotspot's passive crowds. During a sunny weekday in May, he filled about 400 of the 1,600 seats. Willie responded with a remarkable 90-minute show in an intimate setting. Alcohol wasn't served at the theater, but the stage was covered with Jose Cuervo tequila banners.

"There's nothing like Branson," Willie said with a smirk after spending 50 minutes meeting fans. "But it's still like touring to me because the days that I'm off I'll play somewhere else before coming back here."

And what about rumblings that Nelson would bring an unsavory crowd to conservative Branson, where Playboy isn't sold in stores?

"I haven't seen 'em yet. Have you?" Nelson responded. He smiled then said of the matinee show's sedate audience: "They definitely weren't here today."

Steve Ripley, Tractors

—— 1995 ——

In 1981, Ripley toured and recorded as Bob Dylan's guitar player.

"You can't know Bob Dylan. He was a regular guy at times, but he just happens to be some kind of genius. He fulfilled the fantasy of what Bob Dylan should be—writing lyrics on napkins and matchbook covers. He reawakened songwriting aspirations in me."

Marty Stuart

—— 2007 ——

"There are two people you can never count out 100 years from now: That's Johnny Cash and Bob Dylan."

Jason Petty,
Hank Williams impersonator

—— 2002 ——

The iconic Hank Williams, who died at 29 on Jan. 1, 1953, became a country superstar—one who seemed hell-bent on a short life and a lasting legacy.

"And I've been performing as Hank Williams longer than Hank Williams performed," said Petty, then 33.

Williams, an alcoholic who suffered from depression, lost his wife to divorce; was fired by the Grand Ole Opry for missing appearances; and suffered chronic back pain.

"We don't sugarcoat his life in the show. But I'm not going to linger from the first song: (cheerfully) 'Hey, Hank had a drinkin' problem and depression and, good Lord, how did he get up in the morning? Here's another song.'

"I've interviewed every living band member he had. I've talked to his family. These people tell me that 95 percent of the time Hank was your best friend and laughing and jovial. But that other five percent was a living nightmare for him and the people around him.

"I hope my love for the music comes through. I also have kind of a gaunt, thin face and angular features that Hank had. You put the hat and the suit on me and people gasp, 'Wow.'"

Alison Krauss

On this day, she received photos from a recording session with Dolly Parton held a couple of months previously. It remained Krauss' fondest memory. The pair stood two feet apart recording a song for one of Parton's albums. After Parton performed, Krauss sang poorly.

"Dolly had to leave because I was so intimidated. I mean, she's the queen. Forget her fame—she has my favorite voice."

Sara Watkins,
Nickel Creek

— 2005 —

"Dolly is always Dolly. She is who she is. She's always dressed up. She's always incredibly gracious and really funny. She's always been encouraging to us. She genuinely loves music."

CHAPTER 4

Songwriting and Albums

Guy Clark

—— 1994 ——

On his relatively minimal attention: "Of course, it's frustrating, but it's also part of the baggage. I write for me, always thinking about me doing the songs. That's always been my most successful work.

"I have a hard market to target and to reach where you are selling enough albums to really make a difference. I think John Prine does it really well. The audience is there, it's just difficult to access."

John Mellencamp

—— 1987 ——

"I was inundated with people who acted like 'Pink Houses' meant so much to them.

"To me, when I wrote it, it was just another song. Sometimes, I'll write a song and say, 'This is not even honest and I won't put it on the record'—like 'Jack and Diane.' My only number 1 record, and I didn't want to put it on the album, because I didn't think it was honest."

Trisha Yearwood

—— 1994 ——

"The challenge is to make music that can be popular now but also be around in five years.

"The greatest success for me would be for someone to pick up one of my albums in 10 years, play it and say, 'This still holds up well.' That's the way I feel about my Emmylou Harris records and all my Linda Ronstadt albums."

Eric Church

"We have to get back to making great albums and building fans through that process. I know people who have had massive number 1s that I played with a couple of years ago, and I can't tell you where they are now."

John Hiatt

—— 2008 ——

"I never think of casting a song until way after the fact. I mainly just write for the sheer joy of writing songs. It's what I do. I've been doing it since I was 11. It's a part of who I am."

Does songwriting get easier?

"No, no, no. When you start the process, it's the same old thing: Pick up a guitar and sit around strumming. There's always that moment where I feel like I've never written a song before and I don't know how to write a song and stare at a blank page.

"Then, out of all that and the self doubt, something will come, if you're lucky. When you write one, you think, 'This is wonderful. I love writing.' It's a lot of emotion."

He added: "I never set out to get covered. I always look at it as a really cool plus. I'm lucky that it happens. I don't write songs for other people. The times I've tried I've failed miserably. I'm not a made-to-order songwriter."

Iris DeMent

During 10,000 Maniacs' "MTV Unplugged" concert, singer Natalie Merchant and special guest David Byrne performed a cover of DeMent's "Let the Mystery Be."

DeMent said her knowledge of their music is limited, but she understood the significance.

"And it's really, really hard to even imagine."

DeMent wrote the stunning ballad "This Kind of Happy" with Merle Haggard, one of her supporters.

"We were sitting on his tour bus and talking and playing music. He asked if I had any songs he hadn't heard yet. I told him about this one that I'd been working on for a couple years and played it. He said, 'I believe I can help you with that.' Fifteen minutes later, we had the chorus to the song."

She knew the song wouldn't work commercially: "It didn't take long to figure out what the ballgame was for me to get radio airplay. I obviously do not play by the rules. I enjoy doing my music the way I feel it and that's all I intend to do."

Did Merle agree?

She laughed. "Merle told me to do that in language I can't repeat."

Lyle Lovett

Hearing that his haunting ballad "Nobody Knows Me" was played at a wedding:

"It is a cheating song!" He sighed and continued: "But if somebody expresses an interest in one of my songs, I don't try explaining to them why they shouldn't be interested. I draw the conclusion that they don't quite get it. Or who knows, maybe they do. We shouldn't judge the emotional state of newlyweds."

He paused: "I've heard that people play 'She's No Lady (She's My Wife)' at their wedding."

Lee Roy Parnell

— 1992 —

A stellar singer/guitarist, he co-wrote Pirates of the Mississippi's sly and bouncy hit single, "Too Much," with Guy Clark. The song jokingly rattles off lines warning about overindulgence. Parnell expected record company objections to the line, "Too much of you know what'll blind ya."

Turns out, record executives only questioned the line, "Too much cocaine ain't the answer."

"They thought we were saying some cocaine is okay, which is silly. It still made it on the record."

Clint Black

— 1992 —

"I've found that a lot of critics, rather than look at the album 'The Hard Way' and find unique qualities, are quick to compare it to [his debut] 'Killin' Time.' That's a backhanded compliment. I'm going to grow and develop as an artist. 'Killin' Time,' in a lot of people's minds, will never be surpassed, even though I think I'm making better records now."

Mark O'Connor,
instrumentalist

—— 2004 ——

Between 1985 and 1989, O'Connor was Nashville's most in-demand studio fiddle player. He's heard on hits by dozens of acts, ranging from the Judds to Travis Tritt to Randy Travis.

But he shifted to his own compositions as a classical violinist.

"What's happened is violin music has gotten so technically advanced that it is hard to do more than a few things. To learn and master the classical repertoire, modern music and Baroque music is asking a lot."

He continued, "I've been working on my own style for practically my whole life. It's this kind of modern folk-influenced violin playing that has classical and jazz nuances. It makes sense for me to cultivate more music to make this style flourish."

Joe Diffie

Diffie spent nine years working at an Oklahoma foundry and performing in bluegrass and gospel groups on weekends. He moved to Nashville in 1986 after being laid off at the foundry and failing to find another job. Also, his first marriage ended.

In Nashville, he wrote songs for other artists—including Holly Dunn's hit, "There Goes My Heart Again"—but mostly he made a living from working in shipping and receiving at a guitar factory.

"I think I choose some of my songs because of my background. I relate to them. That's where I came from and what I did for so long. They fit my life."

Steve Earle

"I don't think Woody Guthrie was a political songwriter. I think he was a songwriter who lived in politically charged times. I've always had my political beliefs, but these are politically charged times.

"Most people who bought 'Copperhead Road' were disposed Lynyrd Skynyrd fans. There were people who understood why I wrote 'Copperhead Road' and 'Johnny Come Lately.' I was trying to lend a voice to people other than myself. That's why I do what I do."

CHAPTER 5

Defining Country

K.T. Oslin

—— 1990 ——

"When I was a teenager, I loathed country music. It was all sung by old men, who in reality were probably in their 30s but they seemed old, singing about drinking whiskey and cheating on their wives.

"It didn't compute to a teenager. Country music is very adult. Most of all, I think you need to be grown up to really understand what they're singing about."

Mark Chesnutt

—— 1992 ——

As a teenager, Chesnutt played drums in a rock band, performing Van Halen, Ted Nugent and Kiss covers.

After rehearsals, "I would jump in my car and put George Jones and Merle Haggard in the tape player. Yeah, a few friends thought I was pretty strange."

Tim McGraw
—— 1995 ——

"When I open my mouth to sing, it comes out country."

Eric Church
—— 2009 ——

"I still think country music's the coolest format. It's the true home of the troubadour; it's the true home of the singer-songwriter."

Bill Malone, historian

"When I visit my older brother, we like to pick and sing. If I bring in somebody he hasn't met before, he'll ask, 'Is he a hillbilly?' He doesn't mean social status, he means, 'Does he like country music?'

"The music started out as rural, working-class music, but it reaches out to everyone. I think a lot of people are embarrassed to let their feelings show, but country music isn't embarrassed to do that. And that means singing about the death of a parent or a breakup of a love affair or sobbing over a glass of beer in a honky tonk."

Travis Tritt

"If you're upper class, you can enjoy my music. But my music is directed toward a very specific group of people, and it's the majority of this country—the people who keep this country going."

Bill Friskics-Warren, critic/author

—— 2003 ——

Friskics-Warren co-wrote the book *Heartaches by the Number: Country Music's 500 Greatest Singles.*

"I find myself defending the one-dimensional portrayal throughout history of country music and of the country music audience.

"The audience is more diverse than most people acknowledge. But country music is remarkably durable and lasting. In spite of itself, it's been able to evolve and grow."

k.d. lang

—— 1996 ——

"I'm a veggie burger in a McDonald's world."

Martin Zellar, Gear Daddies

—— 1991 ——

Although the four-member band is labeled as a rock group, they have obvious country influences.

"It's a weird Catch-22. I'm a big fan of country music, and I don't mind the association. But if you mention 'country,' it alienates rock people. Then a country fan might say, 'This isn't country.' I always say, 'There's a country flavor to the music.'"

Bill Lloyd, Foster & Lloyd

—— 1989 ——

"Some people check out country from sort of a sideways glance to see if there's anything going on over there that they like."

In 1989, "Nashville has opened its arms to new talent. It seems like somebody woke up and said, 'We've got to keep this genre alive and let all these people in.'"

Randy Travis

—— 1990 ——

After performing for President George H.W. Bush twice, Travis received a personal tour of the White House by the president.

"President Bush said, 'Let me show you this desk back here. This is where I keep my music collection.' He opened a drawer, and there was myself, the Oak Ridge Boys, Patsy Cline and all kinds of country music."

Ray Price
—— 2003 ——

On how he'd like to be remembered:

He didn't hesitate.

"As the best damn singer they ever heard. Is that good enough?"

Phil Humphrey, Fendermen
—— 1995 ——

A singer for one-hit pop wonder the Fendermen, Humphrey recorded with his bandmates a rockabilly cover of Jimmie Rodgers' "Mule Skinner Blues." But Humphrey declined to appear on the Grand Ole Opry.

"Red Foley phoned me in 1960 from the Grand Ole Opry and I hung up on him. I told him, 'I'm not a hillbilly singer.' That's something I've regretted for a long time. He phoned me twice, and I told him to stuff it."

Neko Case

Don't call her an alt-country artist.

"That just irritates me. Why call it alternative country? Why can't it just be country music? The one thing I cling to is that I can call the music that I play country.

"I talked to some major labels when I was younger. Some of them were total liars and creeps and disappeared and thank God they did. I've been approached by other major labels. I'm not saying it's not good for everybody, but it's probably not great for me. I haven't seen a deal out there that I like.

"They don't have to find anybody. They can make people. They're not looking for people like me. I would be too difficult. They would have to send me somewhere where they would get me to sing songs they want me to sing. It doesn't hurt my feelings. I'm pretty happy where I am."

Nanci Griffith

Two performers, Kathy Mattea and Suzy Bogguss, covered Griffith-penned songs—"Love at the Five and Dime" and "Outbound Plane," respectively—with much popular success. Griffith never had her own hit.

"For me as an artist, it's been a blessing to be on the outskirts. It's given me an enormous amount of creative freedom."

In hindsight, she feels fine that her two stabs at becoming a hit-making country artist in the mid-1980s faltered.

"If I had been given airplay on country radio, I think it would have been the end of my career, because I don't really fit in. I'm glad I'm not there."

Marty Stuart

—— 2007 ——

On his success and the genre:

"It looks like one big blessing. It was a dream I had as a little boy, and I've gotten to do what was in my heart. It's still rewarding. But it's never been about the past. It's always about taking the whole story forward."

Mary Chapin Carpenter

—— 1998 ——

Asked if she feels odd being an Ivy League grad, Brown University, in country music circles, she said:

"I'm always offended by that question."

Clarence "Gatemouth" Brown, guitarist/fiddler

—— 2004 ——

Brown appeared on TV's "Hee Haw" in the 1970s and recorded with his friend Roy Clark. In 1999, he donated several items, including his guitar, fiddle and a stage outfit, to the Country Music Hall of Fame.

About to turn 80 years old in 2004, he explained his musical style.

"I play American music. A lot of people are put in certain categories. Not me. I skip all over the place: cajun, country, bluegrass, jazz, blues, calypso and polkas. You name it."

Still, Brown often found himself labeled as a bluesman.

"That's what society wants to do: A Black man needs to play blues or jazz. The hell with society. I play what I want. Yeah, that's right."

CHAPTER 6

Names and Looks

U2 as the Dalton Brothers

—— 1987 ——

During the Joshua Tree tour, U2 performed a sold-out show at Indianapolis' Hoosier Dome. The band's second opening act, Los Lobos, faced travel delays and left a lengthy gap between the first opener, the BoDeans, and U2.

As a result, U2, using exaggerated southern accents, brought out their once-private country alter ego called the Dalton Brothers. Dressed in huge wigs and—for Bono and the Edge—cowboy hats and sunglasses, U2 stepped on stage as the Daltons and performed two country tunes: an original called "Lucille" (not the Kenny Rogers' song) and a cover of Hank Williams' "Lost Highway," sung by the Edge.

More than 50,000 U2 fans didn't know that the raggedy country performers were the iconic rockers. Most of the crowd was indifferent and a tiny handful booed—although a few concertgoers slowly recognized the Daltons, who were introduced as Alton (Bono), pictured below; Luke (Edge); Duke (Larry Mullen); and Betty (Adam Clayton), dressed in drag.

The country quartet Dalton Brothers made only one other public appearance: at a Los Angeles show two weeks later.

Julie Roberts

—— 2005 ——

Her real name is Julie Roberts. Her label asked her to consider changing it because of its closeness to Julia Roberts, who was at the height of her career.

"Of course, I considered that. But my music is honest and keeping my name is being honest."

After an awards show in Las Vegas, her driver held a sign with "Roberts" on it. She laughed. "The driver brought a really nice car because he thought he was going to be driving Julia Roberts."

Jack Daniels,
Highway 101

—— 1991 ——

Yes, Daniels' real name is Jack Daniels.

"It's my dad's name, too."

William Lee Golden,
Oak Ridge Boys

—— 2002 ——

On his beard: The beard is real.

"It's about 21 or 22 inches from bottom lip down."

He grew it after some rugged friends ridiculed him.

"I was a clean-cut guy for a long time. I was a dapper young man. For three or four years, I wore a stubby beard. I used to go camping with some mountain men. They prodded me, 'Hey, boy, won't that beard ever grow any?' I was trimming it once a week. It became a curiosity within myself about what nature really provided here. I got curious about the potential of my beard. I allowed it to grow naturally."

It took almost three years to grow, but it has stopped growing.

"I sat next to ZZ Top's Billy Gibbons [long-bearded] on a flight from Nashville to Minneapolis. It was interesting to see the double takes people took when people stepped on that plane."

Beard details:

"It's certainly not heavy. If I cut it at this point, I would be lost without it. You get attached to something like this. When it was first growing out, I had to learn not to reach over a table if there's a lit candle on it.

"There are also certain foods that you gotta be careful to eat because you can really make a mess in a hurry. Honey and molasses really needs to be washed out of a beard. You can't just wipe it out."

Fans love it.

"A lot of them want to feel it and run their hands through it to see if it's real. I have to have a sense of humor about it myself.

You can't look this way without a little bit of humor. You can't be that serious. There was a time, when I was first growing it out, I'd wake up in the morning, turn on the light and scare myself in the mirror."

Wind can be an enemy.

"Riding a motorcycle really tangles my beard. So does riding in a car with the window open or on the back of a truck. It takes a while to get the tangles out."

Porter Wagoner

His beautifully crafted rhinestone suits were a notable factor in his career.

On wearing the colorful suits:

A rodeo tailor sent him his first flashy suit in 1953.

"It was a peach-colored rhinestone suit that was unbelievable. It had covered wagons, wagon wheels going down the legs of the pants. I couldn't believe it was something to wear. My sister told me she counted 11 times that I took it off and put it on in one day."

Crowds loved it.

"That's when I knew that people want you to look like you're on stage, not just walking in after having delivered milk."

Farm Aid IV

—— 1990 ——

The exact order of appearance, in the early evening, for the 70-act, 14-hour benefit concert in Indianapolis:
Iggy Pop, John Hiatt, Ricky Van Shelton, Arlo Guthrie, K.T. Oslin, Guns N' Roses, Lyle Lovett, John Denver

Jimmy Buffett

—— 2004 ——

To promote the opening of his chain restaurant, Cheeseburger in Paradise, he performed an hour-long charity show there for 200 fans. Another few hundred fans watched and listened through large windows while standing in brutal, sub-zero Wisconsin weather in mid-January. He marveled at their toughness.

"I'm going from here to Hawaii," he told the crowd. "I'll send a car for you."

Chris Thile, Nickel Creek
and Punch Brothers
—— 2008 ——

Told that Nickel Creek bandmate Sara Watkins said his energy is considerable off stage, too, he agreed.

"My self-perception is that I'm fair excitable. In concert, It's 95 percent adrenaline. People expect you to deliver."

Larry the Cable Guy, comic

—— 2005 ——

"When you have something that's hot like the catchphrase 'Git-R-Done,' it does get old. But I know this is going to last a little longer. I started saying 'Git-R-Done' on the radio in Orlando in 1991 and you still hear it everywhere.

"But I mostly bring fans in from rural areas. They're coming in from the farms! There are not a lot of entertainers, especially comedians, who proclaim themselves as conservative and talk about conservative things. I'm hardcore. I'm Ronald Reagan, John Wayne and Ted Nugent all the way."

Eddie Rabbitt

—— 1989 ——

A few hours before two sold-out county fair shows in a small Midwest city, the bearded Rabbitt exercised by jogging through town.

Did anyone recognize him, given that he sold nearly 10,000 tickets?

He shook his head and smiled. "I don't look like Eddie Rabbitt when I'm running."

Boxcar Willie,
Grand Ole Opry member

—— 1990 ——

In concert, Boxcar Willie performed with an eight-piece band called the Texas Trainmen and two background singers dubbed the Hobo Honeys.

How did the singing "hobo" Boxcar Willie develop? In 1976, Lecil Travis Martin, a Nashville DJ and daytime TV host, returned to his first profession: singer. Combining a lifelong passion for trains and a fondness for traditional country songs, Martin developed his character.

Boxcar Willie sold three million copies of the album "King of the Road" through TV commercials on more than 250 stations.

And what about his love of trains?

"God," he said, "never made an ugly train."

CHAPTER 7

Humble and Kind

Alan Jackson

For 11 months in 1985, Jackson worked in the mailroom at cable TV's Nashville Network offices. He received the job through happenstance.

"I moved to Nashville, and I was looking for any day job, whether it was in a garage or whatever. I went into the employment office and they needed somebody to work at TNN."

The best perk? He hung out backstage at the Country Music Awards.

"Everybody was going through, like George Strait and Hank Williams Jr.; I was completely star struck."

Carrie Underwood

"It's hard to set goals because I feel so lucky for all the stuff that's happened so far. I'd feel selfish and guilty to ask for more."

Sebastian Bach,
Skid Row

—— 2008 ——

Bach marveled that Carrie Underwood covered Skid Row's biggest hit, "I Remember You," in concert throughout her 2007 tour.

"It's on YouTube. You gotta see it, dude. It's incredible. She's perfect."

Wynonna

—— 2004 ——

Hello?

Caller: "Tom! It's Wynonna!"

How are you?

Caller: "I'm kicking butt." (laughs) "I'm not going to put up with anything."

Richard Young, Kentucky Headhunters

—— 1994 ——

Young apologized for calling an hour late. He was at his family's farm in rural Kentucky.

"We had a bunch of cows that got out," Young explained, "and I was trying to get the fence fixed."

Kitty Wells
—— 1994 ——

"I hope people remember me as a humble, kind person. I hope, in some small way, I've meant something to them through my singing."

Lyle Lovett
—— 2006 ——

"I always think about trying to do the best I can at whatever I'm doing at the moment. I've approached my life that way.

"From that, good things will happen. It's not a matter of strategy. It's not a matter of where do I want to be in five years. It's, 'What am I doing right this minute? How can I make tonight's show the best it can be?' That's what it's about every day."

Jeff Hanna,
Nitty Gritty Dirt Band
—— 1995 ——

"From 1982 to 1990, everything we put out connected on country radio. We didn't go out of our way to make that happen.

"We played Dirt Band music that was considered country rock or pop in the early 1970s. and country radio expanded to include that music. It gave us a real shot of adrenaline."

Martin Zellar,
Gear Daddies
—— 1991 ——

Immediately after a Friday night appearance on "Late Night with David Letterman," Gear Daddies' lead singer Martin Zellar stood backstage numb and overwhelmed.

"For a second, I didn't remember anything. I didn't know if I sang the right lyrics, if I played the guitar part," he said. "I could have fallen down, and I wouldn't have remembered."

The one-song gig went smoothly, and the Minneapolis-based Gear Daddies received more publicity than a year's worth of club gigs. Amused by the band's name, Letterman repeated it throughout the show.

"The next night, I was singing at my cousin's wedding," Zellar said. "I went from playing to a million people on Friday night to 40 relatives on Saturday night."

CHAPTER 8

Big, Big Hits

Earl Scruggs
—— 2003 ——

On "The Ballad of Jed Clampett":

Scruggs and his Bill Monroe bandmate Lester Flatt, a guitarist and singer, left Monroe's band to form their own group. The legendary Flatt and Scruggs set the standard for bluegrass bands. Their most popular tune, though, is "The Ballad of Jed Clampett," the theme to TV's goofy "Beverly Hillbillies."

"It's pretty amazing, isn't it? But I wonder once in a while how many groups will still be played 50 years from now."

Don McLean
—— 1997 ——

On "American Pie":

"The good thing about 'American Pie' is it's like having a hit every day of the year. It's my tune. It brings people to my body of work.

"The song is meant to be serious and it's meant to be fun at the same time. It's meant to be obvious and it's meant to be mysterious. I managed to achieve what I was trying to accomplish: Capture a certain kind of mood in the record."

Josh Turner

—— 2004 ——

On his first hit "Long Black Train":

"It has that roots element that came from music I grew up on. The first music I heard was bluegrass gospel music like the Stanley Brothers, the Osborne Brothers and southern gospel quartets. People think it's an old song. Then they realize, 'Wait, I've never heard that.'"

Kathy Mattea

— 1994 —

On "Where've You Been":

Co-written by Mattea's husband, Jon Vezner, the ballad describes a couple's loving relationship into old age.

"I remember thinking, 'I can't imagine radio playing this song on morning drive with people going to work.' I thought it was too heavy, too emotional."

Kitty Wells

— 1994 —

In 1952, Wells—then 33 and the mother of three—recorded "It Wasn't God Who Made Honky Tonk Angels," a response to Hank Thompson's hit "The Wild Side of Life." The song pointedly put the blame on men who cheat on their wives.

"To me, it was just a song I was singing, but it really hit people." She paused. "It didn't pertain to my way of life."

Ray Price

— 2003 —

The Kris Kristofferson-penned "For the Good Times" provided one of Price's signature songs. The tune's adult-themed lyrics could be interpreted as a man trying to sleep with a woman after their relationship ends.

"I know, I know. You can take it any way you want. It depends on the guy." He laughed. "I don't think of that anymore."

Steve Ripley, Tractors

—— 1995 ——

"The power of a hit single is amazing. People in Pocatello, Idaho, scream when we play 'Baby Likes to Rock It.' It makes you scratch your head."

Amy Grant, Christian music star

—— 2004 ——

Grant, who married Vince Gill in 2000 and did a Christmas tour with him, on her crossover pop hits, including 1991 number 1 singles "Baby Baby" and "Every Heartbeat":

"I was definitely making a concerted effort to just broaden the base of what I was singing. I wasn't changing my personality. Faith doesn't just operate in a bubble.

"I delivered songs that were applicable to what was happening on the radio at the time. I don't look back and think, 'Oh, that was the best music I ever made.' There are certain things that have to be working for you if you're pursuing that high visibility—and youth is one of them."

Porter Wagoner

—— 1994 ——

On Whitney Houston's version of Dolly Parton's "I Will Always Love You," which he produced for Parton:

"It's fine, but it's not real," he said. "Whitney has a wonderful voice, but I'm not listening for voice gymnastics on a song. I like heart and feeling."

Darryl Worley

—— 2003 ——

"Have You Forgotten?"— a pointed ballad backing U.S. military force—became one of the quickest singles ever to reach number 1 on the country charts.

"I never thought when we wrote it that it would even be recorded. That's the truth. It's kinda in your face, you know. It's pro-military and pro-American. I'm not a war hawk. No one in their right mind wants to see a war. But sometimes we don't have any choice."

Lee Greenwood

—— 1991 ——

A 1984 hit, "God Bless the USA" was written the year before by Greenwood, who felt despondent about international events, including American hostages being held in Iran.

"I've always tried to express the feeling of the population with my music. When 'God Bless the USA,' was put down on paper, I was making a statement: We have to put the negative feelings of Korea and Vietnam behind us. We needed to turn our attention to being positive and acknowledging that we should be proud of who we are. The line, 'I'm proud to be an American,' probably hadn't been said in 40 years."

Before Greenwood recorded the song, he knew he had a hit.

"I did it onstage night after night two weeks before going into the studio, and it was obvious that it struck an emotional chord with the audience. The lyrics were right, and the people let me know it. It was very moving."

Becky Hobbs

On co-writing Alabama's "Angels Among Us":

"'Angels Among Us' has been the biggest blessing in my career."

The song developed from scary premonitions Hobbs had in the years preceding Jan. 25, 1986. In a van with her bandmates that night after performing at a police benefit in Albertville, Alabama, the group stopped at a red light in hard rain.

"I was sitting in the back on the left side, and our road manager, Randy, was driving. As I looked out the window, I saw an 18-wheeler barreling toward the intersection. I felt Randy lift his foot off the brake so I yelled, 'Stop!' Randy slammed on the brakes. The truck's air horn blasted, then it crashed into us. Time slowed down. Everything was dead quiet. I didn't know if we were dead or alive. It was surreal.

"The truck hit our van's front-left side, but it was totaled. Our trailer, full of equipment, was ripped off as our van spun around on the wet pavement. None of us were severely injured; just cuts and bruises. I had a sprained ankle. Randy said that my yelling 'stop' made him stop. He never saw the truck. A split second difference saved our lives, the police said."

In a bizarre twist, the police officers who arrived on the scene said that they led Ricky Nelson and his band to the airport in Guntersville, Alabama, a few weeks before. That plane, heading to Dallas, crashed killing Nelson and six others.

"After the van accident," Hobbs said. "I felt that the voice that night was my guardian angel. After all, that's what angels do; they bring messages. I wrote down, 'I believe there are angels among us' in my notebook. I savored the idea and jotted down lyrics on and off for several years. It wasn't until Christmas 1992, when I was sitting in my dad's old chair while visiting my mom in Oklahoma, that I got the strongest feeling I had to finish the song immediately.

"When I got back to Nashville, I called co-writer Don Goodman. I said, 'Don, I have this idea, and want to know if you wanna help me finish this song.' I wanted something universal. I played Don what I had, and he had tears. He jumped in, and we finished it."

Tim McGraw

— 1995 —

On "Indian Outlaw," his first hit single, which he didn't write:

"It's just a cute song. It's being taken way too seriously. There have been countless songs you can dissect to death like that. You've got to look at the meaning of the song—or the overall no meaning of the song."

CHAPTER 9

Connecting

Alan Jackson

—— 1992 ——

A Georgia native whose mother was married at age 16 to a 19-year-old man, Jackson let his band do rock covers if the club owner asked for it. But he never sang rock, letting other band members step forward. The 6-foot-4 Jackson stuck to country music, something he knew he could deliver with passion.

"It's hard for someone to walk out there and sing a serious ballad and give off energy. But that's country music. You can do that. You can reach people without banging on the kick drum."

Alison Krauss

—— 2000 ——

"We've got a pile of styles. We had that song 'When You Say Nothing At All' that did well on country radio a few years ago, but I wouldn't categorize it as country. And I don't think of it as folk. We are singers of sad, beautiful songs."

Arlo Guthrie

The acclaimed folk singer-songwriter ("Alice's Restaurant" and Steve Goodman's "City of New Orleans") provided his perspective on the turbulent 1960s:

"What's glorified about the '60s isn't the most interesting part of it. The most interesting part to me is that it was really a revolution of sorts and a very successful one. That's completely overlooked. What's overblown is what we were wearing, what we were listening to.

"That's the least important part of what was going on. But the activism, the willingness of average people, especially young ones, to get out on the streets and demand that the world change and stop doing ridiculous things—whether it's war, whether it's how to treat people, whether it's civil rights, whether it's pollution—that's important."

Pamela Gadd, Wild Rose

— 1990 —

Gadd doesn't understand Wild Rose's comparison to an '80s rock group. "I wouldn't know the Go-Go's if they walked in. I'm about as ignorant about rock as they come."

Wild Rose, an Academy of Country Music nominee for best new group, is one of the few all-female country groups with a major-label record contract.

"We thought an all-female band would be marketable and help us get a record deal. It's something unique. But a gimmick sounds like we're trying to trick people. And calling us a novelty makes the music sound fluffy, and we hate that. We're aggressive. We're hard-driving players."

John Mellencamp

— 1987 —

After appearing before a U.S. Senate subcommittee with Farm Aid organizer Willie Nelson in 1986, Mellencamp realized how corporate farming would squash family farming. The senators seemed uncaring to this development.

"Fourteen senators were scheduled to be there and only six showed up. This one guy, a corporate farm lobbyist, came in, saw Willie and me and said, 'If you're not going to do some pickin' and singin', I'm just going to leave.'"

Peter Yarrow,
Peter, Paul and Mary

—— 1992 ——

On the morning between the trio's Saturday and Sunday night concerts in Springfield, Illinois, Peter Yarrow, Paul Noel Stookey and Mary Travers flew to Washington, D.C., on Sunday morning to perform at the Choice March, an abortion rights rally. A plane took them back to Springfield in time for the group's 7 p.m. show.

"We're proud," Yarrow said, "of the fact that we are legitimate advocates of the positions we espouse."

And the rigorous schedule? "We'll sleep on the flights."

Kix Brooks, Brooks & Dunn

— 1994 —

A record executive matched then-unknowns Kix Brooks and Ronnie Dunn, the second person paired with Brooks. The duo maintained low expectations. Brooks had been a veteran song-writer whose solo career stalled; and Dunn performed on a regional club circuit, based in Oklahoma.

At the time, Brooks, then 35, and Dunn, then 37, seemed unlikely to reach stardom. Linked initially as songwriters while pursuing solo careers in Nashville, Brooks & Dunn had Arista Records dangle a recording contract in front of them on one condition: that they become a duo. In the years before the offer, Brooks wrote a string of hits, including Highway 101's "Who's Lonely Now," and released two unsuccessful solo albums.

The laidback, 6-foot-4 Dunn was a veteran honky-tonk singer. The pair accepted Arista's deal with hesitation, although Brooks admitted: "This was my last shot at chasing my enter-tainment dream. Both of us were so familiar with failure. I had written songs for 10 years in Nashville and I had seen every career scenario go upside down, including a couple of my own."

Larry Frank, concert promoter

— 1995 —

Frank Productions promoted one of Brooks & Dunn's first arena headlining shows: a sold-out concert at a 6,500-person capacity venue in La Crosse, Wisconsin, in early 1994. It's a fond memory.

"Brooks & Dunn wouldn't leave the building after the show. They stood on that stage after all the people were gone and looked out at the seats and reflected on the wonderful night."

Les Paul

Gene Autry introduced him to Colleen Summers, who later changed her name to Mary Ford (pictured below with Paul). They became music partners and were married in 1949.

"I was in Hollywood to do nine shows of country music. I told Gene I need a girl singer to help the show. He said, 'Well, I have a trio of singers and one [Summers] is very talented but shy.' Gene gave me her phone number and I called her. She had told someone her favorite guitar player was Les Paul and she thought someone was joking with her when I called."

Jeff Tweedy,
Uncle Tupelo

—— 1994 ——

Formed by Tweedy and Jay Farrar, Uncle Tupelo developed in the duo's hometown of Belleville, Illinois, a blue-collar city 30 miles from St. Louis. The band's debut album, "No Depression," earned a four-star review from Rolling Stone magazine. Later albums—"Still Feel Gone," "March 16–20, 1992," produced by R.E.M.'s Peter Buck, and its last release "Anodyne"—watched the band evolve from a rollicking outfit to one that likes to take a deep breath during each number.

"I can see how it seems like a total about-face," said Tweedy, 26. "But we feel like we've been doing the same thing all along. Even before we recorded 'No Depression,' we had tried out pedal steel players for the band and we had been doing acoustic shows."

Billy Ray Cyrus

—— 1992 ——

Nothing hit country quicker than Cyrus' "Achy Breaky Heart." Less than three months after its video debut, the song propelled the Flatwood, Kentucky, resident to major fame. At St. Louis' Riverport Amphitheater, the five-act Young Country Roundup—featuring Trisha Yearwood, Brooks & Dunn, Suzy Bogguss, Sammy Kershaw and Cyrus—provided hysteria for the latter act.

Fans on the massive venue's lawn spotted Billy Ray shooting baskets at a hoop in the roomy backstage—and screamed for him. His arrival on stage created the kind of enthusiasm among the crowd that was similar to five-figure lottery winners.

At one point, Cyrus addressed the adulation.

"Excuse me, ma'am," he said pointedly between songs, "but how would you feel if I kept yelling at you to take your shirt off?"

Oh, Billy Ray, grin and bare it.

Later, he played "Achy Breaky." Twice. Why not?

After the second time, Cyrus stood with his fists ready like a boxer while the crowd cheered wildly; as if Billy Ray wanted to tell his detractors (that's you, Travis Tritt) to get in the ring.

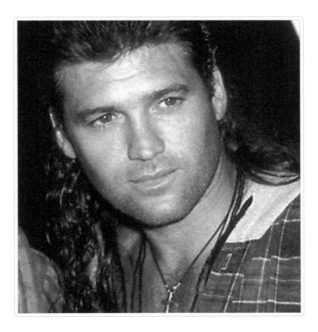

Reed Strom,
Billy Ray Cyrus impersonator
—— 1995 ——

In a show with Elvis Presley, Garth Brooks and Vince Gill impersonators, Reed Strom as Billy Ray Cyrus resembled his character the most out of costume.

When "Achy Breaky Heart" initially hit in 1992, Strom said, "Strangers, little kids, everyone told me I looked like him."

In 1993, Strom met Cyrus before the real Billy Ray's show in Sioux Falls, South Dakota. They talked about show business, and then posed for pictures together.

Strom added: "At one point, Billy Ray asked my mother with a smirk, 'Did you ever meet my dad?'"

Bill Lloyd,
Foster & Lloyd
—— 1988 ——

Lloyd and Radney Foster wrote songs together at a publishing company's building.

"Neither of us had air conditioning at our apartments. One of the reasons we were hanging around there a lot was just to stay cool."

Big Kenny and John Rich, Big & Rich

—— 2005 ——

John Rich said, "We probably have a bit of yin and yang in our personalities."

Big Kenny added, "But the common denominator is that we were both raised with an incredible work ethic. We bring different things to the table. But, when you put the two of us together, it's rocket fuel."

Tim McGraw

McGraw's father is former big league pitcher Tug McGraw. Tim, though, did not meet his famous father until he was 11 and they didn't form a relationship for another eight years after that.

"I'm more like his big brother," McGraw said with a laugh. "He'll come out on the road with us for five or six days. He's enjoying my success."

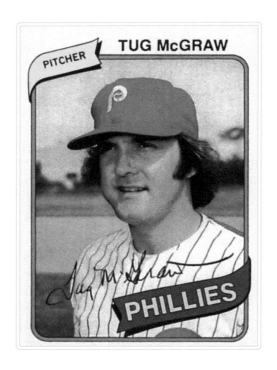

CHAPTER 10

Hardships
and Tragedies

Doc Watson, guitarist

— 2003 —

With two children, Doc and Rosa Lee Watson moved into their own residence in 1953 with Doc, blind since age one, playing guitar but making very little money. Was it a tough life?

"It was. But, you know, the first years we lived out on our own, I'd give every bit of my savings if I could live those four years over. There's something about peace and contentment that no financial security can ever cover. I'm getting philosophical with you. But I know. I've been there.

"The only thing I regret is that I was handicapped and couldn't help with the hard work that my little sweetheart Rosa Lee did to help us along through those years."

He paused. "I'm getting down to the nitty gritty of it. No blowing up stuff about who Doc Watson is to me. I'm one of the people like you and everyone else who has a job."

In 1964, Watson's sighted teen son, Merle—who learned guitar from Watson's wife and his mother Rosa Lee—became Doc's onstage partner. They enjoyed worldwide touring even when folk music's popularity waned. Then in 1985, with their career still flourishing, Merle died in a tractor accident. He was 36.

"I canceled the tour that was coming up after Merle's death. Then, in a dream I had about Merle, he rescued me from a dire situation. I think God sent him to me to show that I couldn't quit. My family came first over my hurt. I had to grit my teeth and face the storm of my heartaches."

Watson called his booking agent and asked him to reinstate the scheduled tour's last show—and then add more shows.

"If you knew Merle well," he added, "you had a friend."

Joe Diffie

Discussing the darkest time in his life: his father's 10 years in prison for a 1972 kidnapping in Eau Claire, Wisconsin:

"It's something everyone regrets. The family was really hurt by it. But my dad has turned his life around. He had a 180-degree turnaround."

At the time, Diffie was 13 and living in tiny Whitehall, Wisconsin. His father, Joe Sr., and another man kidnapped the teen son of an Eau Claire dentist. They released the boy unharmed after receiving a $50,000 ransom. Diffie's father was caught after using some ransom money, which had been marked, to pay a bank loan.

Diffie's family lived in Whitehall from the time he entered sixth grade to his sophomore year in high school, when his family moved to Oklahoma.

"It certainly wasn't an easy time," says Diffie, who stayed in touch with his father. "I take life as it comes and try to go on. That's all you can do."

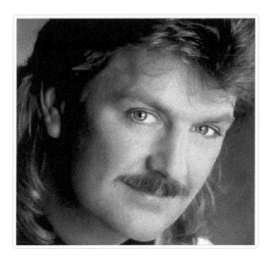

Randy Travis

—— 1990 ——

At age 11, he started drinking and using drugs. Three years later, he drank alcohol daily and continued doing drugs. By age 16, he had been arrested "a lot," he said, for breaking and entering as well as trying to outrun police officers.

Before his last court appearance, the 17-year-old "totaled" four cars, and his lawyer told him during the hearing: "I don't believe I'm going to be able to do something this time."

Then the judge took pity on young Randy Travis. Still shy of voting age, Travis had been performing five nights a week at a North Carolina nightspot called Country City USA. With Travis holding a steady job, the judge opted to release him rather than place the lanky youngster in a juvenile detention center.

"The judge said, 'If you come back before me, son, bring your toothbrush, because you're staying,'" said Travis, 30.

Reflecting on those troubled teen days, Travis paused and said directly: "I don't know why I'm living."

Earl Scruggs

About his childhood:

"We had a little cotton crop, but we were raised very poor. We lived way out in the country. We didn't have electricity, so I didn't have a radio until I was about 15 or 16 years old."

Steve Earle

Three drug overdoses. Two pistols in his face. Three horrifying car wrecks. Five ex-wives. A month-long jail stint. That's Earle's ugly past.

Earle should be dead; he admits that. But those experiences keep him working at a frantic pace now, restoring his pre-drug addiction legacy as one of the finest contemporary songwriters.

"When you don't have to go out and find $500 worth of dope every day," Earle says with a snarl at his sordid history, "it seems like you have a lot of time."

So Earle writes, tours and records. All the time. He's remained drug-free. During that time, he's recorded six acclaimed albums and written a short-story book and a play about an executed Texas woman.

Earle regrets his "lost years" to drugs, adding, "I was age 35 to 40—that's prime time."

To continue that work, Earle knows he must fight his drug demons that nearly killed him.

"I guess I'm supposed to be here. I've stayed around long enough to get clean. But I still go to meetings and call my sponsor. That's how I stay clean. If I stop doing that stuff, you know, I'll be back where I started and I'll die."

Billy Walker

On Patsy Cline's plane crash:

Walker was scheduled to be with Patsy Cline on the plane that crashed in 1963 and killed all four on board. "The Lord would just not let me get on that airplane," he said softly.

Walker and Cline shared an advisor, Randy Hughes, who was the fatal crash's pilot. They were in a multi-act benefit show in Kansas City when Walker received word of a family emergency in Nashville. Another country singer, Hawkshaw Hawkins, gave Walker his commercial plane ticket to Nashville. Hawkins then took Walker's place on Cline's ill-fated flight.

"I was initially listed among the dead because they didn't know we switched," Walker said. "It was heartrending. I felt it should have been me. You never understand why it wasn't you."

Charlie Dick,
Patsy Cline's widower
—— 1996 ——

Dick met Cline at a dance in the 1950s, and they went on their first date—"Friday the 13th, April 1956," he said—while she was separated from her first husband.

"The next day, she was going to be on a TV show, but her car wasn't working. I told her I'd drive her, but I had a wrecked car, too. I had to hustle up my buddy's car to take her."

It wasn't until 1961 that Cline's fame skyrocketed. Dick and Cline's marriage—rocky at times, Dick admitted—was enhanced when he toured with her for two years. Dick, however, had returned to Nashville a day early when Cline played a Kansas City benefit show before her plane crashed.

Dick has five grandchildren; one granddaughter, named Virginia after Patsy's real first name, was killed in a car accident.

Now Dick promotes theatrical productions of Cline's life.

"I've seen eight different people play Patsy. I remember seeing the show for the first time a couple years ago. It was very touching, very good. When everything went black, I thought it was over. Then there's a final scene when Patsy emerges from the darkness in a white suit to sing again. That was very emotional for me."

He paused, cleared his throat and took a deep breath. "That was a grabber."

Donnie Van Zant,
38 Special
— 1992 —

When he helped form 38 Special in 1977, he turned to his brother, Lynyrd Skynyrd vocalist Ronnie Van Zant, for advice.

"I had been through so many different bands, and I was at the edge. I didn't know whether I wanted to continue with music or go to work at a railroad company. I asked Ronnie, 'Should I stay in the music business or go with the security in the railroad business?' Ronnie winked and smiled and told me: 'Man, you've got music in your blood whether you know it or not, and you owe it to yourself to go for your dream one more time.'"

A short time later, Ronnie died in a plane crash. And 38 Special finally hit its popular stride in the early 1980s.

CHAPTER 11

In Concert

Trisha Yearwood

—— 1994 ——

On stage fright during her career's start:

"I called myself 'The Singing Stick.' I didn't move on stage."

Doug Gray,
Marshall Tucker Band

—— 1995 ——

Playing small clubs:

"I put out no less just because you can see the back wall. I enjoy being on stage. I enjoy the excitement that we're still around."

Describing longtime fans:

"People who have been with us this long definitely aren't fans anymore," he said, "they're friends."

Molly Scheer,
Molly & the Heymakers
— 1995 —

Molly & the Heymakers experienced the extremes of touring.

Scheer mentioned a free show in 1993 before nearly 50,000 people in Seattle's Kingdome, where they opened for Travis Tritt and Reba McEntire.

"It went really well. The funny thing is you have those highs like that—those incredible jobs. Then you turn around and you're on a tiny stage in some really small county fair the next night. But we appreciate any gig."

Ranger Doug,
Riders in the Sky
— 1988 —

"At any show—if you stand on stage with big cowboy hats and sing harmony—you're going to have people who want to hear 'Tumbling Tumbleweeds,' 'Cool Water,' and 'Back in the Saddle Again.'"

Wynonna

Becoming a solo artist:

"The demons I was fighting at first were personal. There were inner voices saying, 'You're going to fail. You can't do it without your mom.' I was caught up in the uncertainty: Can I do it? I listened to the fans and they loved me even when I didn't love myself. You did witness it on stage."

Jeff Tweedy, Wilco

After playing three laid-back, country-flavored tunes to start the show, Wilco's frontman heard one restless concertgoer standing near the stage shout, "Play something that cooks."

Tweedy repeated the request, smiled and said, "First, you've got to mix up the recipe."

George Jones

Jones proved guilty of shameless promotion in concert. After the second song, he talked about his own brand of dog and cat food, which sat in bags across the stage.

Kenny Chesney

Playing large venues:

"My band and I knew our lives were changing. This wasn't us at the county fair. This wasn't us in a theater. People came to see us just like they came to see our musical heroes. I played a couple of amphitheaters where I saw Aerosmith and Jimmy Buffett play. I was one of the guys out there partying on the grass. I look out there now and think, 'There's a lot of me out there.'"

He continued: "We've been able to get our hands on some songs that people could really sink their teeth into. A record label can't make fans go to the show then leave and tell others how good it was."

Tanya Tucker

—— 1996 ——

With her band on stage at the outdoor festival Star Spangled-Celebration in Richland Center, Wisconsin, everything seemed set for an entertaining set by Tanya Tucker before 11,000 fans.

Only one problem: Tucker wasn't at the country festival yet.

Her six-piece band and road manager traveled by bus from a previous night's gig in Branson, Missouri; Tucker and a personal assistant flew from Branson to Madison. She arrived in Madison, but Tucker never reached Richland Center—about 60 minutes away—in a rental car in time for her 6:30 p.m. gig before headliner Dwight Yoakam.

Expecting a last-second arrival by Tucker, her band played anxiously on stage for 35 minutes—without Tucker—before festival officials canceled Tucker's set. Tucker's road manager even stood along nearby Highway 14, expecting to spot her. She never arrived.

Alabama

—— 1994 and 2004 ——

A request from the band's detailed tour rider: 50 assorted Tootsie-Pops.

Alabama said goodbye with the foot-stomping style and professionalism that marked the band's grand career in its 2004 farewell tour.

In June 2021, the band began a new yearlong tour . . . to celebrate its 50th anniversary.

Jo-El Sonnier

—— 1990 ——

Sonnier and his firecracker band performed the first of two shows earlier that night, then returned to see only 90 or so people in a facility that comfortably seated nearly 1,000. Everyone sat in the first three rows; behind them, it looked like an empty church.

No one would have blamed Sonnier to smile meagerly, perform a brief gig and make a beeline with his accordion to the tour bus. Instead, he ripped into an inspired and furious hour-and-45-minute set and moved around the stage like a guy in a heated racquetball match.

By the time Sonnier delivered a sizzling encore cover of the Blasters' "So Long Baby Goodbye," the overjoyed crowd witnessed one of the most stellar rock workouts—by a guy with an accordion, no less.

Sarah Buxton
—— 2007 ——

From the concert preview:

"The county fair's headliner is country singer Bucky Covington, a finalist in last winter's 'American Idol,' and he will draw screaming female TV viewers. But newcomer Buxton is the real idol here. She's like Trisha Yearwood mixed with Melissa Etheridge—and she also has songwriting talent to burn.

"Mainstream country radio hasn't given Buxton that breakthrough single yet. As a result, her debut album release has been delayed. She wrote Keith Urban's hit 'Stupid Boy,' but Buxton's version packs more punch.

"Who will be around in a year or two? Covington or Buxton? Vote Buxton."

Alan Jackson
—— 1998 ——

If country star Alan Jackson was any more laid back, he'd tip over on stage. The singer stays close to the microphone stand as if clinging to a life preserver. When he does step away, Jackson doesn't walk, he saunters. Yet, he's always the coolest guy in the room.

Doc Watson

—— 2003 ——

"A good audience," Watson said, "makes an old tune fresh."

The concert's vibe extends beyond eyesight, Watson added.

"It's something you don't have to see. If you feel the spirit there, I know it as good as anyone seeing. To play for a good audience is like good fellowship. It's like several hundred handshakes amplified from one good handshake."

George Strait

—— 2001 ——

After Saturday's Milwaukee encore of "Cowboy Rides Away," Strait spent 15 minutes on the stage in Miller Park's deep centerfield shaking hands and signing autographs for fans while his band played. It was a sincere gesture, one that meant far more than an arsenal of fireworks.

Dixie Chicks
—— 2000 ——

Dixie Chicks' tour officials sent this message to promoters:

"The DIXIE CHICK fan base for 2000s Fly tour is approximately 70 percent female. Therefore the possibility of overcrowded female restrooms exists throughout the night. We can remedy this overcrowding by turning around some of the men's restroom facilities in the main concourse into women's facilities. This is not mandatory but just a suggestion."

Aaron Tippin

Country music muscleman Aaron Tippin described negative blue-collar stereotypes as created by people "who are afraid to get their hands dirty."

So, in concert while he performed one song with a wireless microphone, he assembled an entire bicycle then gave it to a local charity.

Hank Williams Jr.

Hank Jr. slowed down his raucous concert once. He sat alone, playing wistfully on guitar, while a photo montage of his father, Hank Sr., appeared on two big screens. The final photo showed Hank Jr., at age 3, placing a wreath on his father's grave at the funeral. In the crowd, 10,000 hearts broke.

Shania Twain

For two hours, she charmed the crowd, playing the part of everyone's big sister rather than a video vixen. Despite wearing black leather pants and a tiny vest and sporting humongous hair, she never used the stage to tease anyone.

This was a family show—youngsters filled the arena—and Shania reached out by inviting kids and teens onstage as well as using nine members of a children's choir during "God Bless the Child."

She also promoted a local food bank, describing, in a rare personal moment, about experiencing hunger during her difficult childhood.

Kitty Wells

Two weeks after suffering a bleeding ulcer, Wells, about to turn 75, finished the third of 10 shows in a five-day stint at Wisconsin Dells' Country Legends Music Theatre. She performs with her husband of 57 years, Johnny Wright, and her son, Bobby Wright. Her grandson plays drums.

Still, why not choose a well-deserved retirement?

"Oh, no. As long as my voice holds, I'll keep working. When you're working, you feel like you're doing something special. A lot of people, when they quit working, they don't stay around very long. It seems like they don't have anything to live for."

Johnny Cash

He opened with the fiery "Folsom Prison Blues" then played the roots rocker "Get Rhythm." Before saying, "Hello, I'm Johnny Cash," he delivered two other classics; took off his long, black jacket; rolled up his sleeves; and looked like a western gun-slinger who stepped into the saloon.

Best of all, his voice still commands the same attention as an approaching train. In concert, Cash wasn't content to be a museum relic.

Merle Haggard

At 56, Haggard looked older on stage. A few feet away from the club's stage, his souvenir t-shirts screamed the inscription, "The LEGEND Continues," almost as if teasing.

Then it changed. Shortly into his 20-song set, Merle settled in and inspiration flowed. Packed spur-to-spur, the club's capacity crowd of about 600 created enough noise to rouse Merle from performance slumber. Once he felt it, Merle squeezed the sentiment from his vintage repertoire, including "Silver Wings" and "Mama Tried," followed by a chestnut "Old Man from the Mountain." Legendary indeed.

Ralph Stanley

— 2001 —

Thirty minutes before the opening act played, headliner and bluegrass legend Ralph Stanley stood at the souvenir stand. Stanley, 74, took money for his CDs, t-shirts and videotapes from fans—then signed each item.

It was a remarkable sight, and one that spoke volumes about how bluegrass stars must scratch and claw for every dime on the road.

What did Stanley think of the Coen brothers' film "O Brother, Where Art Thou?"—featuring two of his songs and another tune strongly associated with him?

"I liked the movie," he said with a huge smile, "but I loved the soundtrack."

CPSIA information can be obtained
at www.ICGtesting.com
Printed in the USA
BVHW092102161121
621776BV00023B/863